Chook

About the Authors

Dr. Gerloch retired in 1999 from a career as academic and research scientist in the field of quantum chemistry in the University of Cambridge. He is an Emeritus Fellow of Trinity Hall. He and his wife, Gwyneth, have since lived in Canberra, Australia. During his first twenty years of blissful retired domesticity, Malcolm has enjoyed gardening, house renovation and above all, learning to cook in several cuisines. Gwyneth has relinquished the kitchen with mixed feelings. Prior to writing (mostly) children's books, Malcolm's greatest achievement has been the construction of a dual-manual harpsichord for his wife to play. That was a present to thank her for introducing him to the non-scientific literature of – mostly – the nineteenth and twentieth century European and twentieth century North American writers.

About the Illustrator

Nina has formally studied graphic design, marketing, advertising, and communications. She is passionate about visual communications in particular and also dabbles in art and craft - including watercolour painting, weaving, stitching, knitting, drawing, calligraphy, and lettering. Her other passion is pottery, and she enjoys making functional tableware with tactile satin-matte glazes in natural colours inspired by native Australian flora. Nina is based in Canberra where she grew up, and she has a soft spot for the Bush Capital.

Gwyneth Gerloch and Malcolm Gerloch
Illustrations by Nina Davis

Chook

Nightingale Books

NIGHTINGALE PAPERBACK

© Copyright 2021
Gwyneth Gerloch and Malcolm Gerloch
Illustrations by Nina Davis

The right of Gwyneth Gerloch and Malcolm Gerloch to be
identified as author of this work has been asserted by them in
accordance with the Copyright, Designs and Patents Act 1988.

All Rights Reserved

No reproduction, copy or transmission of this publication
may be made without written permission.
No paragraph of this publication may be reproduced,
copied or transmitted save with the written permission of the
publisher, or in accordance with the provisions
of the Copyright Act 1956 (as amended).

Any person who commits any unauthorised act in relation to
this publication may be liable to criminal
prosecution and civil claims for damages.

A CIP catalogue record for this title is
available from the British Library.
ISBN 978-1-83875-190-6

Nightingale Books is an imprint of
Pegasus Elliot MacKenzie Publishers Ltd.
www.pegasuspublishers.com

First Published in 2021

Nightingale Books
Sheraton House Castle Park
Cambridge England

Printed & Bound in Great Britain

Dedication

To Stephen Rouch for his many years of care.

Growing Up

The trouble was that when Pat and Ron Miller gave their young son, Terry, the honour of naming the latest member of their hen-house, they had not yet explained to him that all of their fowl except the rooster were hens; that is, female. But Terry had insisted that the newcomer be named Stevie and he just wasn't going to change his mind. He'd chosen that name because his best friend was called Steve. Actually, he was called Stephen but that was almost always shortened to Steve. The only concession his parents could extract from him was that the bird's name be spelled, Stevi. So Stevi it was. In fairness, Stevi herself was perfectly relaxed about the spelling of her name. It turns out that this unusual naming might have caused a degree of confusion in the poor bird's mind. But that's for later. By the way, Terry also got to name the family dog a couple of years back. He was Terry's dog really. He'd been given the dog on his seventh birthday. Coll was a beautiful collie with a light and dark brown coat on his back and a creamy-white chest which was everyone's pride and joy.

Meanwhile, Stevi, the chook, had lots of things

to get used to in her young life: five other hens, older and wiser than herself; a hearty and – she thought – dominant rooster; Coll the dog; and, of course, the whole Miller family itself.

But one of her very first lessons was learning to pick up her food. Her Mum would come close to her, cluck a bit, and pick up some pellets of food in her beak – or sometimes, some seed – and then drop them on the ground in front of Stevi. Then Mum would do it all over again until Stevi got the idea and picked up the food herself. Trouble was, Stevi copied Mum by dropping her food right back on the ground! Mum was very patient, though. After all, she had taught all her other offspring how to eat and she knew that Stevi would get the point eventually. And she did.

As Stevi grew up, she did all the other things she was expected to do, things she learned from several older hens in the Millers' garden. In due course, she learned how to scratch the ground, how to lay eggs and how to be friendly towards Old Bill, the rooster, how to cluck and how to forage for food around the place. She would look all over the garden for any easily reachable fruit or vegetables, any seeds, any worms or insects and creepy-crawlies in general. The garden was large and the Millers were only too happy for their chooks to wage war on all the disagreeable insects, slugs and snails they could find.

Ron Miller had built a hen-house for their chickens but it was not gated in any way so the birds could come and go as they pleased. The hen-house was there to provide a warm, dry place for them to sleep, to roost, and to lay their eggs. The only confining barrier was a wire-netting fence all around the boundary of the garden, often concealed just behind long stretches of hedging or small trees. Otherwise, these lucky chooks had an enormous area in which to rummage. The Miller home was at the end of a long lane outside of a small village. They were very nearly in the countryside. Certainly, their large garden was surrounded by a local farmer's fields.

It was during one of her earlier explorations of the garden that Stevi first came across ants. Her attention was caught by a long trail of these tiny insects crossing her path from, it seemed to her, one side of the garden to the other. Stevi's eyesight was pretty good and she could see that each ant hurrying across her path was only about five millimetres long but that there were thousands of them in four – in some places six – streams. Half of these worker ants were crossing from right to left while the other half were going in the opposite direction. It was rather like watching traffic on a six-lane highway. Not that Stevi had ever seen traffic on a highway, six-lane or otherwise. She was quite fascinated and looked more closely at what seemed to be going on. One thing she did notice was that, somewhat away from these unending streams of ants marching past, were a small number who just hung around, occasionally moving a little way parallel to the main force, and then, moving back. They just seemed to be hanging around. Were they lost? Were they objectors to the big march? Were they on a "demo"?

Stevi also noticed that these particular ants were rather larger than the thousands of workers busily marching along. They were the guards; soldiers, whose job it was to protect the workers streaming by. They moved back and forth a little as they kept an eye out for danger, but while there was none, these guys had an easy job.

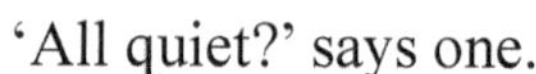

'All quiet?' says one.

'All quiet,' the other imaginatively replies.

The workers had been to a patch of rotting fruit and fungus which they wanted to build their nest with and to feed their queen, and each worker had collected a considerable amount of the fungus and fruit to carry away. Of course, that morsel was only a few millimetres in size but when you remember that there were thousands, indeed tens of thousands, of these little workers all doing their bit, you can see that a considerable amount of food and building material would get back home to their nest. Their underground nest would be several metres across by the time it was finished and it could be home to a million or more of these creatures. Stevi couldn't see the nest, though, which actually wasn't in the garden but in a field outside.

Sometime before Stevi had begun looking at these marching workers, a solitary ant had gone foraging for food. He had no idea where to look but he had a good sense of smell so he would find something interesting if he stumbled near it at random. That was his job. Go forth and seek. Eventually, he had found a good patch of the sort of food he and his fellows like. Maybe a piece of rotting peach or apricot.

Hey! Don't turn your nose up. Everybody has to

eat and it's good that all that good stuff doesn't go to waste.

Anyway, his job then was to rush home and tell everybody else where it was and how to get there. So, as he ran home, he sprayed what we might call a scent (its proper name is a pheromone), so leaving a trail as straight as he could, all the way back to the nest.

'I've found some!' he would say to his fellows. 'I've laid a track.' The workers could detect this scent very easily and they just followed the smelly trail all the way to the food. There, each took some of the fungus or fruit, or a leaf maybe, and followed the trail back home. But the scent gradually evaporated away – if it didn't, the whole world would be criss-crossed with smelly trails and the ants would be hopelessly confused and they don't want that, do they? – so the returning workers left some more scent to reinforce the trail so that all their fellows would continue to find the food and get it back to the nest. Clever little things, aren't they?

We might listen in to their conversation as the outward-bound lines of ants pass their inward-bound colleagues.

'Hello, Tony!' says one.

'Hello, Tony!' another ant replies. 'Good day, Tony.'

'Good day, Tony!'

They're all called Tony, of course, because they prefer the shortened form of Ant-ony. After all, it would be silly to be using up all their energy saying:

'Hello, Antony!'

'Hello Antony!'

wouldn't it? And they wouldn't want to abbreviate Antony to Ant because if they said, 'Hello, Ant!' it might sound as if they were greeting their auntie; you know, like:

'Hello Aunt!'

These things have to be worked out properly.

Actually, this is only half the story, of course, because half the workers are female. They are called Ant-oinette but it would be too much to greet each other with:

'Hello, Antoinette!'

'Good day, Antoinette!'

So that gets shortened to Toni. Now we have greetings like:

'Hello, Tony!,' 'Hello, Toni!' or 'Good day, Toni!,' 'Good day, Tony.'

Nothing could be simpler, really.

Do you like doing sums? Well, even if you don't, try this. Suppose that ant trail from their nest to their food is ten metres long. That might be a quarter of the way across Stevi's garden, for instance. And suppose those ants are five millimetres long. That means that each ant has to march ten metres divided by five millimetres, times its own length. There are one thousand millimetres in a metre (that's why it's called a millimetre). So each ant marches ten thousand millimetres divided by five millimetres, times its own length; that is two thousand times its own length. Now think of the dog, Coll, who is, let us say, one metre long. An equivalent journey for Coll would be two thousand times its own length or two thousand metres; which is two kilometres. Now the ants probably make their journey in five minutes. Can Coll run two kilometres in five minutes? Maybe. But the ants do their journey, collect some food, and march straight back home. And then, they do it all over again; and again; and again… Maybe they should be called Bolt rather than Tony!

Not only do they march quickly, and for huge distances if necessary, ants can also carry up to twenty times their own weight – again, for long distances. The reason why they're so strong is that, instead of having heavy bones inside their bodies to lug around as we have, they have lightweight exoskeletons; "exo" means "outside". So like crabs, for instance, their "bones" are in the form of lightweight but amazingly strong, hollow shells on their outsides protecting their guts and stuff inside. Altogether, therefore, ants are very light for their strength so they can run fast and far, and carry heavy things.

By the way, there are probably about a thousand million, million ants in the world; roughly one million ants for every human being. Put it another way: the total weight of the world's ants is roughly equal to the total weight of the world's human beings. *Fant*astic!

Where were we? Oh yes! Stevi had just come across these trails of ants. She'd never seen ants before and she hadn't actually googled them yet on her smart-phone, so she didn't know all that stuff about what they ate and how strong they were. She just followed her instinct and dipped her beak into the six-lane highway and hoovered ten or twenty ants up into her mouth. Like millions of chickens before her, she discovered that she rather liked the taste of ants and she hoovered up some more. Nature can be cruel, but you must remember that we all have to eat.

After a while, Stevi wandered off and looked for her next course; in this case, some corn seed which Ron Miller had dropped the day earlier. And so her day proceeded. The sun was out and she was content and she was growing up.

Damaged Fencing

Ron Miller had a lot to do around his garden: lots of flowers and fruit trees to prune; lots of vegetables to plant, and when they were just small seedlings, protect from the chickens; he had to cut the grass, though young Terry often did that; and, oh! So many things. It was so difficult to make sure that everything was done on time or even at all, sometimes. Just take that wire-netting fence all around the outer reaches of the garden. That was there to keep the chickens in, of course, but also to keep any enemies out. The trouble was that much of the fence lay behind shrubs and trees so it wasn't easy to see if it was damaged. You certainly couldn't see from far away. You had to walk right up to the garden boundary and push some shrubs aside so that you could inspect the wire netting. This wasn't something that Ron would do every day, or even every week, but maybe he should have done it every month or so. Well, he hadn't, and a hole had appeared behind one of the shrubs. He soon found what had made the hole, as we shall see.

Late one evening, Coll was curled up in his basket outside on the verandah. That verandah went all round the house but Coll's basket was always to be found just outside the back door. The sun had set and it was quite dark out there, not that Coll noticed because his eyes were shut. He wasn't totally asleep yet but he was well on the way.

Stevi was still wandering around the garden some way from the house, although all her sisters – and even the rooster – were quietly tucked up on the straw in the hen-house. Stevi should have been in her bed too but she had heard something outside and was curious. Suddenly, she saw a monster rushing towards her at high speed and she squawked loudly and repeatedly in terror. She had never seen a fox before and the way things were going, she might not see one again.

Stevi ran and fluttered towards the house where Coll was trying to sleep. The other chickens were awakened by Stevi's calls for help and began calling out as well. Then Bill, the rooster, joined in and made an enormously loud noise. Roosters can really do that.

Coll couldn't sleep with all that racket going on and he woke with his eyes wide open almost as soon as Stevi began screaming. Coll saw the fox in an instant and ran towards it at full speed, barking for all he was worth. He saw how the fox was about to grab hold of Stevi and, quick as a flash and without any care for his own safety, Coll ran in between the fox and the terrified chicken. The fox immediately changed its target and went for Coll with all the ferocity that wild animals have and domestic animals do without. It was an uneven match, even though Coll was a good-sized collie and still in the prime of his life. The fox managed to get Coll's left hind leg in his mouth and had caused a nasty and bloody wound.

Fox and dog were racing round each other. Coll was barking fit to bust and Stevi was clucking and yelping wildly. Bill kept calling out enough to waken all the neighbourhood, if there had been any neighbours, that is.

There was so much noise that Ron left off watching his favourite TV show and came rushing out of the house to see what all the kerfuffle was about. He saw the red fox straight away and, picking up a heavy walking stick he kept on the verandah, chased after the fox and began to beat it with the stick to stop it attacking Coll again. The fox hissed but now recognised that it was outnumbered and beat a hasty retreat. Ron chased after it and saw it disappear through that hole in the wire netting fence. By this time, Terry and his mum had both come out to see what was the matter and when they saw how badly Coll was bleeding, Pat ran up to him, carried him in her arms and wrapped him in a towel. Terry chased after Stevi and carried her and stroked her until she calmed down a bit. Everybody was shaken up by the attack.

'Come and look at Coll, quick!' Terry shouted to his dad, but Ron insisted on repairing the hole in the wire fence immediately,

'Otherwise the fox may come back and get the other chickens,' he shouted. He found a piece of spare netting and wired it over the hole until the fence was secure again. Only then did he come in to see how the dog was doing. By this time, Coll was much calmer but his leg was very badly gashed and still losing blood.

'We must get Coll to the vet immediately,' said Ron, 'and see about stitches for that wound. I don't like the look of that one little bit.' Pat was stroking Coll who was panting hard, and Terry had come into the kitchen carrying and stroking Stevi who was still making upset noises. Only when Stevi saw Coll did she quieten down. She was obviously very upset about Coll. Well, everybody was, of course.

Ron called the vet to warn him that he was bringing in a wounded dog and then carried Coll, still wrapped in the towel, to the car and drove off to the surgery. Poor old Coll. He didn't at all like the vet poking him and cleaning the wound in his leg. But he didn't mind his sewing up the gash with six stitches because, by then, he had been injected with a local anaesthetic. He didn't feel that at all, thank goodness. The vet told Ron to keep Coll warm and to spoil him for a few days while his wound healed.

'He was lucky,' he said.

It was an hour and a half later that Ron brought Coll back home and put him into his basket, still outside on the verandah because it was summer and warm out there. Pat had put Coll's food and drink bowls next to his basket with some treats to tempt him. Coll drank some water but didn't feel up to solid food, though. Ron, Pat and Terry all gathered around Coll's basket for a few minutes while he settled, before leaving him in peace.

Sometime after they had gone inside, Coll heard the pitapat of Stevi's feet as she climbed onto the deck of the verandah. She came right up to Coll and made some very quiet clucks. She picked up a morsel of Coll's food in her beak and then dropped it back in his bowl just as she had been taught when she was very little. She did it again but Coll just wasn't interested. Then Stevi gently pecked on Coll's side and clucked some more. Coll fell asleep then, exhausted but happy.

But Coll was not happy when Terry popped out to him early next morning. Coll tried to move but clearly found it difficult. More than that, he showed no interest in his food and that was not at all like him. Terry reported the situation to his mum and dad and Ron came out to have a look for himself. He felt Coll's head which seemed rather warm and touched his nose which was definitely dry.

'I think Coll's running a temperature,' announced Ron, 'We'll leave things alone for the morning but we must keep checking.'

By lunchtime, matters were no better. If anything, Coll seemed more sick and miserable.

'I'm going to 'phone the vet again,' Ron said.

'I don't like the sound of that,' the vet told him. 'I have to call into the Taylor farm in half an hour. I'll pop in on you on the way and have a look at Coll.'

He was as good as his word and checked Coll's temperature with a thermometer stuck up his bottom. Coll didn't seem to mind but Terry was a bit embarrassed.

'Yes,' the vet said, 'he's running quite a temperature. I think Coll must have been infected by germs from the fox's mouth. That's only too common with fox wounds, I'm afraid. Of course, we don't know exactly what the infection is, so I shall give Coll a broad-spectrum antibiotic and we'll see how that goes. It will take a couple of days to see real improvement, I'm afraid.' He injected Coll with a drug he took from his bag and gave Coll a pat of reassurance.

The Millers just had to wait. Coll remained poorly and very quiet for the next two days while first Terry and then his mum tried to tempt him with some of his favourite food. But Coll wasn't interested.

Stevi climbed up onto the deck several times to see how her friend was doing. She put her head on his for a while but Coll didn't move. Stevi slowly went away.

Terry was getting worried now. Stevi wasn't the only one who loved Coll. After two days of this, and seeing no improvement in Coll's condition, Ron called the vet again. When the vet re-examined Coll, he announced that the antibiotic he had given didn't seem to be working.

'Coll really is very poorly indeed,' he said. 'I'm worried. I'll give him an injection of a new drug. It's very powerful but I can't guarantee that it will work, I'm afraid. I'll pop in tomorrow morning and check on him again.'

Everyone was very worried about Coll by this time. Nobody said the words but each member of the family had the same thoughts.

'Are we going to lose Coll?'

For the rest of the day, Coll's temperature seemed to rise even more. What did that mean? As everyone went to bed that night, after saying goodnight to Coll, they really began to believe that their beautiful collie dog would die in the night. Terry was very quiet and in tears as he said goodnight to his dog. Coll had been so brave but that fox had got him. Stevi climbed up onto the deck again that night and quietly pecked at Coll and put her head on his.

Terry rushed out to see Coll as soon as he woke next morning.

Coll was not only alive but was moving around the deck – only slowly, but even so – and had clearly eaten some of the food in his bowl.

'Mum! Dad! Coll's getting better!' shouted Terry as he ran full speed back into the house.

Pat and Ron rushed outside to see for themselves. Yes! Coll was definitely much better. By the time the vet arrived later in the morning, Coll was almost back to his old cheery self. He wasn't running anywhere, of course, but he had wandered round the house for a while before going out into the garden. He was wagging his tail as he began looking for Stevi. When she saw him, she began clucking wildly. She just wouldn't stop. She went up to Coll and pecked at his ear – gently, of course – and clucked some more. Coll licked Stevi's back.

'I guess that's all right then,' the vet said. 'I'll just check his temperature and feel around a bit, but I guess he'll be all right from now on.'

And he was. Each day, Coll got stronger and stronger and, after a while, he began running round the garden at high speed and asking to go off for long walks outside.

'I thought we'd lost him,' Ron said one day. Nobody said anything but they all thought the same thing. The vet had saved him but it had been a close call.

A Settled Time

Life returned to normal eventually and peace reigned for days, for weeks and months, and then years. Everyone grew a little older but life at the Miller household was happy and healthy.

Coll and Stevi had become inseparable. Yes, they each did their own things, obviously, because Stevi couldn't run like Coll, and Coll wasn't too keen on eating ants or snails or slugs. But when the end of the day came and it was time to go to bed, Coll lay down on his side in his basket and was soon joined by Stevi who crawled into the gap between his front and back legs and settled herself down in the warmth of Coll's tummy. Coll would lick her back for a while before putting his head down for the night. Sometimes, when the Millers had friends round for an evening meal, they would quietly take them out onto the verandah so they could see Stevi nested in Coll's tummy. Their friends were amazed but Coll and Stevi found the whole thing totally natural.

During the daytime, Coll and Stevi often played together. Stevi had taken to jumping up onto Coll's back so that he could take her for rides round the garden. It was a hilarious sight to see a chook clinging to the back of a collie while he ran all over the place. Sometimes, Stevi would even make two jumps; one taking her onto Coll's back, and a second, up onto his head. He didn't seem to mind one bit. Yet again, visitors to the Miller family would take out their phones and take pictures. Nobody would have believed them otherwise. If Coll should carry Stevi up to the chicken coop and her sister hens were in residence, there would be a round of approval as all chooks clucked loudly and long. But none of the other chickens tried to cadge a lift from Coll. They all seemed to understand that the friendship between Stevi and Coll was unique and very special.

Meanwhile, Terry, who was now eleven years old – getting on for twelve – started hankering after a tree house. There was a lovely old oak tree near the bottom of the Miller's garden which branched into a fork of three thick branches about three metres above ground level. It seemed to Terry to be an obvious place to build a tree house.

'Oh! Please, Dad, can we build one?' he implored Ron Miller.

After a little of 'We'll see' and 'It'll take a long time' and stuff like that, Ron agreed to build it.

'But you must help,' he said.

Well that's exactly what Terry had hoped for. He had seen some drawings of tree houses in one of his books so that he had already formed an idea of how it should look. Actually, he had drawn up some plans in his sketch-book and he showed them to his dad.

'Could it be something like this?' he asked and continued, 'We could use those old planks at the back of the garage for its floor and roof and maybe some of those fence posts to make the walls. What do you think, Dad?'

Ron was quite impressed with Terry's drawings. He hadn't yet considered how he would build it and he thought that Terry's ideas could well be useful. You're never too old to learn and Ron was big enough to recognise that.

Ron discussed every detail with his son as they made preparations. Ron was a wise dad. They knew they couldn't build the complete house on the ground because they would be unable to lift it into position and, in any case, it was surely a good idea to fasten different parts to the tree branches as they went along. More than that, because the tree branches met in an irregular fork – after all, the oak was a living tree, not some factory-made support truss – they would have to modify Terry's drawings as they went along.

They began by making the floor of the tree house out of some old planks of wood which Terry had seen leaning against the back wall of the garage. These planks were held together by nailing strong pieces cut from old fencing posts across them. Ron did that bit because they used ten-centimetre-long nails which took a heavy blow to hammer home. The size of the finished floor was easily large enough for four young lads to sit on.

They tied some heavy rope around the floor section and, using a stout ladder, threw the end over a high but strong branch. When they tried heaving on the end of the rope to lift the floor section into place, they found that they just didn't have the strength. That floor was just too heavy. Pat always said that Ron built things like a tank.

'Not to worry,' said Ron, 'I'll ask a couple of my mates to give us a hand. This will be the only part of the whole thing as heavy as this.'

So he called his friends on the phone and they agreed to come round on Saturday morning, which was only two days away. Terry was really itching to get going but he had to learn a bit of patience.

Ron's friends were as good as their word and they arrived just after 9am bringing some extra ropes and a pulley system with them.

That pulley was a brainwave because it meant that they could heave the heavy floor section up into the fork without scraping a deep gouge into the branch above. And anyway, it's far easier to turn a pulley wheel than to rub against a knotty tree branch. It all took some time to set up and they had to be very careful that nothing could break as they did the heavy lifting because that would have been very dangerous. It was nearly half past ten before everything was ready. Ron's two strong mates began to heave on the rope while Ron and Terry carefully guided the floor section into the triple fork of the old oak tree. After all that long wait, it all went very smoothly and the floor was sitting, more or less in its final position, in less than five minutes.

The problem now was to fasten the floor firmly in place so that it was as nearly level as possible but, more importantly, so that it was absolutely firm and could take up to four boys, if necessary, moving about on it without it moving or falling. That was something that Ron and Terry had foreseen but couldn't plan in detail, simply because of the odd shape of the three-fold fork in the tree. But they had a rough plan in mind and soon fastened sturdy supports all round the floor section and even drilled large holes in the floorboards so that sturdy ropes could be passed through them so as to tie the floor in place as well. All that took about an hour and a half but by the time they were finished, Ron announced that the floor could support a tank.

Then Pat came out of the house with some drinks. So that was all right. After a while, Ron's truly wonderful friends left as the rest of the construction could be done by Terry and his dad on their own. They planned to take several days over it so there was no great hurry. It didn't take Pat too long to persuade them to come inside the house for lunch. They must have been working hard for they were ravenous and had second helpings. Pat knew they would.

In the afternoon, Ron and Terry climbed up their

ladder onto the floor they'd spent the morning fixing. It was fine and strong. You could tell. Nothing moved or swayed. So they brought up some lighter pieces of wood to make frames for the sides and end of the tree house. They had already worked out how they would do all this from Terry's sketches and it wasn't difficult. The idea was to make these frames in outline, carry them down to the garage, and then to cover them with overlapping facing laths in such a way that when it rained, the water would run off from these laths without getting the inside of the tree house wet. A lath, by the way, is just a thin, flat piece of wood which need not be very strong because, here, it is just used for covering the wooden frame of the treehouse. By overlapping a higher lath over a lower, rain will run down the outside, instead of getting inside, the house. They left holes in each side for windows so that Terry and his friends would be able to look out in all directions.

Terry was impatient and wanted them to keep building until they fell asleep on the job, but his dad said that they must be patient.

'Rome wasn't built in a day,' he said.

Terry pondered this remark but couldn't quite understand it. Anyway, Ron saw to it that they made headway each day; steady progress without getting exhausted. By bedtime each evening for the next ten days, Terry was really tired and fell asleep as soon as his head hit the pillow. Eventually, he dreamed of flying up to a tree house in the sky with Stevi. Or, anyway, that's how he remembered the dream when he woke in the morning.

At last, the tree house was finished. It had a pointed roof just like the roof of the family home, except that this one was covered in a sort of tarred felt which kept the house waterproof without the great expense of a proper roof like the family house. There were windows in each side and in the door, which was part of the last side to be constructed. And, finally, they had made a strong ladder so that it was easy for Terry and his friends to climb up to his new, special garden home. Terry was absolutely delighted. It had turned out to be pretty much like his early drawings. And it was dry inside.

And it was HIS! He was so pleased and he gave his dad a big hug.

It was then time to show it off to Coll and Stevi. Actually, Stevi got there first. Chickens can't fly very far but they can fly a bit if they really want to. And Stevi really wanted to. She made a real effort and flew up through the open door and onto the floor after Terry had climbed up for the umpteenth time so that she could be with him in his new den. She clucked a lot and walked all around the inside, looking at every nook and cranny. She really seemed to like it. It probably felt a bit like the hen house to Stevi. Terry told her to wait a minute and climbed down the ladder. He called Coll who came running. Terry lifted him up in his arms and carried him up into the tree house where he was greeted by Stevi with more clucking and pecking.

Terry invited his friend Steve into his new home. Steve liked it a lot and they began to spend more and more time there together. Terry had a collection of little carving tools he had acquired over the past few years and he decided to keep them up there. When he was on his own, he would spend many happy hours carving little figures of various animals he had either seen live or on the TV. He enjoyed showing these to Steve. In turn, Steve would bring a growing collection of fossils he was gathering together. His prize possession was an ammonite about twenty centimetres across. Steve loved the spiral shape and googled to find out as much as he could about them. Terry had been given an old, somewhat battered pair of binoculars a couple of years earlier and he decided to keep them up there in his tree house. Being that high up and having those binoculars meant that he could see a long way over the fields of the farm which surrounded the Miller home. Farmer Taylor's farm was mostly arable and all the fields which surrounded Terry's home were sown with wheat or rape and stuff. That tree house had been completed during a lovely warm summer and many of the fields around them were showing the vivid yellow colour of rape. But the Taylor farm did have a few cows and Terry could clearly see those in the distance with his binoculars.

While he was on his own up there, he carved several model cows for his collection.

'What do you want to be when you grow up?' Steve asked Terry one day.

Terry knew immediately. 'I want to be a vet,' he said. He never forgot how the vet had saved Coll's life all those years ago. Well, it was only three years ago but it seemed much longer than that to Terry. 'What about you, Steve?' Terry asked.

'Oh, I want to be a doctor,' Steve replied with equal certainty. They were so sure about these things.

It had been a lovely quiet summer. But there was trouble yet in store.

Stop the Thief!

It was on one of those blissful nights which a good summer brings when, quite late and with everyone inside and outside the house asleep, that Stevi, settled into Coll's tummy as usual, felt tremors on the deck of the verandah. They were slow and very gentle but Stevi, with her acute sensitivity, felt them immediately. She could sense vibrations from a long way away. She kept very quiet but opened her eyes to see what was causing them. She could just see, in the darkness, a man, a stranger, carefully creeping along the deck towards the back door of the house. Stevi didn't recognise the man and was sure he was no friend. The man was carrying a bag and when he reached the back door, he gently turned the knob.

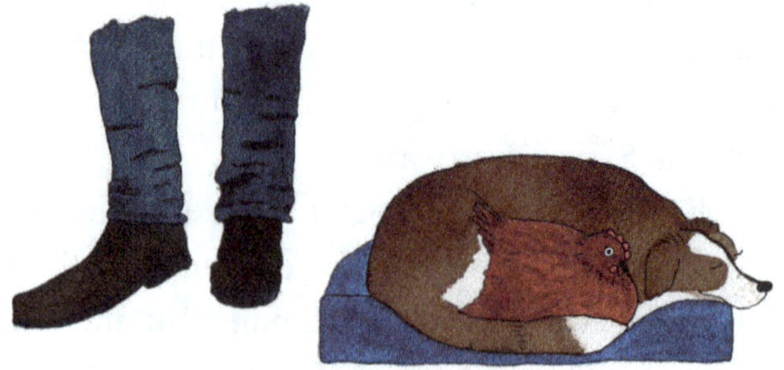

The Millers lived some way out of a village – some would say they lived in the country almost – and never locked their doors. So this burglar, for that was what he was, had an easy job that night. He crept inside, closed the door quietly behind him, and began looking for anything of value that was worth his taking.

Jake Moody had been a thief for most of his life. He had even been a thief as a little boy. Growing up hadn't improved him. He had been caught by the police on two occasions and had served one term in prison. But with experience and care, he had become a pretty efficient thief. He stole regularly but hadn't been caught for many years. He had learned not to be too greedy. He only stole things he could carry on his own for he trusted nobody to join him in his robbing. He only took small, but preferably valuable, objects that he could put into his bag and carry off to sell somewhere. So cash, smart-phones, cameras and silver objects like cutlery, mugs and picture frames were the sort of things he took. He always stole at night when everyone was asleep and he had learned to move around very quietly. As far as Jake was concerned, tonight was a thieving night like any other.

Stevi felt it was time to act. She began shuffling up against Coll's tummy; she gave him some pecks on his face; but she was careful not to make any sound. After a while, Coll woke up, wondering what all the movements were about. Stevi climbed out of the basket and went towards the back door of the house. Coll looked at her without any understanding. So Stevi ran back to Coll, gave him a couple of pecks, ran back to the house door and waited. Coll slowly got to his feet and left his basket. He ambled up to the door and gave Stevi a lick on her back. He still didn't understand what Stevi was on about and began to walk back to his basket. Stevi jumped up into the air, fluttering her wings. Coll stopped and looked at her. She jumped up again with more wing flutterings. Coll returned to where she was standing and looked at her. She went quiet for a few moments. Then Coll heard it. It sounded like a drawer being opened and closed. It wasn't very loud but then he could just hear someone moving around inside the house. There were no lights to be seen except for a mere pinpoint of light moving all over the place. That was the burglar's penlight torch, of course.

Jake stopped what he was doing for a moment. Had he heard a noise outside on the deck? He listened for some moments but there was nothing so he went back to his searching for loot. He had already found a couple of silver picture frames and put them into his bag. He knew that when he got home, he would remove the photographs inside those frames and throw them away, but he had no time to spend on that right here while he was "on the job". He also knew that sometimes picture frames were engraved and he didn't want those. They could be traced too easily by the police and, as we know, Jake had learned over the years to be a very careful thief. But here was not the place and now was not the time to search for engraving marks. He'd do all that when he got home. If he had to throw engraved picture frames away later, that was just tough luck, but he was disciplined enough to do it.

The thief moved from one room to another, pausing to listen from time to time before rummaging in cupboards and drawers. He was lucky. He found a rather good camera. That would bring a good price, for Jake knew exactly where to sell these things. He would like to have found some jewellery. Sometimes ladies would leave a pair of earrings on a sideboard, or maybe a bracelet. Not tonight though. They had obviously been taken upstairs to the bedroom. A long time ago, Jake had decided not to stretch his luck too far and risk waking anyone. Some people are heavy sleepers. Nothing seems to awaken them. But others are light sleepers who might wake up if a fly landed on their noses. Jake did not believe in taking silly risks. He prided himself on being a professional thief. It's interesting how even thieves have their pride. So Jake Moody stayed downstairs that night. He'd been in the place for about three quarters of an hour now and his bag was probably half-full.

'That's enough,' thought Jake, 'that'll do,' and he began to return to the back door of the house. He'd just open the door quietly as he had done hundreds of times before, and he'd be away and off home for a good kip.

Coll didn't know what to do when he first heard the intruder. He and Stevi just stood outside the back door, wondering. It had gone quiet inside the house and that funny little light seemed to have disappeared. The burglar had moved on to another room from which Coll and Stevi could hear nothing. But they stood their ground, more in uncertainty about what they should do than anything else. It was quite a long while before they heard the burglar returning to the back room and the back door. He quietly opened the back door.

That was when Coll realised what he should do. He jumped up at the stranger and barked as loudly as he could and wouldn't stop. Stevi jumped up and down, clucking wildly. All that hullabaloo woke the other hens and the rooster too. And, of course, once Bill, the rooster, started off with his very noisy cock-a-doodle-do calls, everyone in the house woke up and lights were switched on all over the place. Jake decided to make a run for it but Coll ran round and round him, trying to bite his legs and trip him up at least. He didn't really succeed in preventing Jake from moving away from the house but he most certainly slowed his progress. But that was when Stevi came into her own. Stevi jumped up and flapped her wings very hard and managed even to flap them into the burglar's face. Stevi was squawking fit to bust. And she struck lucky that night.

That was because careful Jake Moody, the burglar's burglar, was one of those people who just cannot stand flapping feathers anywhere near him. He was a pteronophobe – which means someone who has a fear of feathers. (By the way, you pronounce that as "teronophobe"; the "p" is silent, as in bath.)

Ha! Unlucky, Jake! He just froze in total terror. He couldn't move a muscle apart from his mouth which kept shouting something about, 'Get this something-or-other bird outa my face.'

Stevi kept up her attack and Coll kept running round and round Mr. Moody, barking furiously. By this time several of the other hens were approaching. But far worse for friend Moody was Bill, the rooster and boss of this parish – and you'd better believe it – springing up into his face and sounding off as only a cockerel can. You'd have to feel a little sorry for Jake for a moment. Maybe not. Served him right; he shouldn't have gone out thieving.

Jake remained rooted to the spot as Ron Miller came outside and grabbed him by the arms, dragging him back into the house. Truth to tell, Jake Moody was more than a little relieved to be captured by a mere human and to be hauled away from those frightful birds. While Ron stood over the cringing burglar, Pat telephoned the police and explained that they'd caught a burglar red-handed and could the police hurry up and get round here immediately. Or sooner would be even better.

About half an hour later, P. C. Knewall arrived in his police car. Pat took him into the back room where Ron was standing over the burglar who, by this time, had no fight left in him. He just wanted the whole thing to be over and to be taken somewhere where there were no feathers.

'Oh! It's you, Jake,' said Constable Knewall. 'Long time no see.'

Obviously Mr. Moody was well known to the police. Knewall looked at Moody's bag.

'I see you've come equipped, as usual.' He turned to Ron Miller and continued, 'You've done well to catch him red-handed, sir. Jake Moody is usually pretty quiet and slick. He's normally far away before his victims wake up. How did you manage it? Are you a light sleeper? Were you disturbed by some noise?'

Well, Ron Miller was certainly disturbed by noise but most of it came from creatures other than Jake Moody. Ron began to tell the story – or as much of it as he could guess. P. C. Knewall assumed that it was the collie dog who had apprehended the burglar. That was a natural assumption, after all. He turned to Coll and patted him on his head.

'What a good dog you are,' he said in his most patronising tone. Coll ignored him but then yelped at Stevi who jumped up onto Coll's head and fluttered her wings. Ron told Knewall:

'I think the real hero tonight is Stevi here. She had the burglar frozen with fear. He obviously cannot stand to be near anything with feathers.'

'Are you serious?' asked the policeman. 'Jake Moody, no less, was apprehended by a chicken.'

'That's about the size of it,' Ron assured P. C. Knewall.

'Well, I do apologise,' said the policeman. He turned to Stevi and said, in the most serious tones he could manage, 'Well done, chicken, I shall report your bravery to the chief.'

'Her name is Stevi,' Terry said.

'Whose?' asked the constable.

'The chicken's,' replied Terry. 'Make sure you get it right in your report.'

That was a bit cheeky, I suppose.

Other books in this series

Bird
Bahs
Flea

Other books for juniors by Malcolm Gerloch

Rosie 'N' Co.
Zada
Spike

Other books for seniors by Malcolm Gerloch

Old Harald and Other Stories

www.ingramcontent.com/pod-product-compliance
Lightning Source LLC
Chambersburg PA
CBHW061102050726
47592CB00004B/1789